Volume 13
I Am a Child of God

**A year's worth of simple messages
that can be given in church
or family home evening**

Volume 13
I Am a Child of God

**A year's worth of simple messages
that can be given in church
or family home evening**

Heidi Doxey

**CFI
An Imprint of Cedar Fort, Inc.
Springville, Utah**

ISBN: 978-1-4621-1141-1

Published by CFI, an imprint of Cedar Fort, Inc.
2373 W. 700 S., Springville, Utah, 84663
www.cedarfort.com

Cover design by Erica Dixon
Cover design © 2012 by Lyle Mortimer
Edited by Michelle Stoll

Printed in the United States of America

10 9 8 7 6 5 4 3 2 1

To David and Joanne Doxey for their legacy of
true discipleship, hard work, and charity.

I love you, Nana and Gramps.

Contents

Introduction   ix

Chapter 1:   **God Is My Father and He Wants Me to Return to Him**   1

Chapter 2:   **I Came to Earth to Live with God's Children**   7

Chapter 3:   **Jesus Christ Prepared the Way for Me to Return to God**   13

Chapter 4:   **The Church of Jesus Christ Is on the Earth Again**   19

Chapter 5:   **We Learn about the Restored Gospel from Prophets**   25

Chapter 6:   **Being Baptized and Confirmed Is Part of God's Plan for Me**   31

Contents

Chapter 7:   Heavenly Father's Plan Includes
             Eternal Families   37

Chapter 8:   I Can Talk with God When I Pray   43

Chapter 9:   Heavenly Father Wants Me to
             Serve Him Always   49

Chapter 10: I Can Share the Gospel
             with Everyone   55

Chapter 11: We Should Be Grateful   61

Chapter 12: Someday Jesus Christ Will
             Return to the Earth   67

Introduction

This year in Primary, we will learn about what it means to be a child of God. Our Heavenly Father loves us because we are his spirit sons and daughters. He created a wonderful plan for us that will help us to return to him someday. I know that it can be hard to feel like a child of God when we live in such a troubling time, but that is exactly why we need to remember our divine heritage and the great potential each one of us has to become like our Heavenly Father and his Son, Jesus Christ.

This book is a great resource when you need to write a talk for Primary—especially at the last minute—but it can also be used in family home evenings, sharing time, in your Primary class, or for individual study. Discussing the principles in this book as a family will bring you closer together.

Each talk includes five different elements: a story, a scripture, a visual aid, a list of suggested illustrations, and a thought question. You can also find additional resources for each talk online at TinyTalksBooks.com.

Story

Heavenly Father has given us many examples in the scriptures and in our own lives that illustrate what it means to be a child of God. We need to practice applying these examples to our own lives. This is a necessary skill for salvation and one children can learn early. The stories in this book come from the scriptures and from real life. As you read them, encourage your children to think of other stories that incorporate the topics in the lesson. Nephi tells us that we need to "liken all scriptures unto us" and that this will benefit us and help us to learn from them (1 Nephi 19:23).

Visual Aid

In addition to a story, each talk includes a reference to a visual aid. Most are from the Gospel Art Book (GAB). This resource is available online and can be an excellent helper. If you wish to purchase your own copy of the Gospel Art Book, it is available through Church Distribution Services. Another option is to personalize the talk by having your children illustrate it themselves.

List of Illustrations

With each talk, you will find a list of suggested illustrations that complement the story. This is especially useful for children who are too young to read the talk themselves. By having your children color their own pictures of the things discussed in the talk, you will help them remember the concepts they learned as you also encourage them to share their talents. Some of these illustrations repeat in later talks, so you may want to keep your pictures handy to use again later. In this way your family can build your own personal art kit to use in family home evening and other settings. In years to come, this will be a treasured resource and will bring back many good memories.

As a family night variation, before the lesson begins, you could have the children take turns drawing the illustrations while everyone guesses what the picture is. Once all the pictures have been drawn, have the children guess the topic of the lesson by looking at the pictures they've drawn.

Thought Question

Finally, each talk includes a thought question. These questions are specifically geared toward older children and teenagers, though with a little parental prompting, they can also be appropriate for young children. These questions will help you to include your whole family in discussions and talk preparation. They can help you all delve a little deeper into the doctrine behind each story. As you discuss these topics, make sure your children have a chance to express their thoughts. You may be surprised by how much they have already learned about the gospel.

Song Ideas

A list of song ideas is included at the end of this book. Most are from the *Children's Songbook,* with a few from our adult hymn book. For each tiny talk, you will find at least one song that corresponds to the themes and ideas presented that week. For young children especially, music can be a wonderful way to reinforce and expand on key doctrinal concepts. Learning these songs when they are young will give your children a solid foundation to rely on for years to come. Even if your own musical abilities are limited, you will find joy in singing with your children and in sharing with them the precious gospel truths contained in the lyrics.

In addition to the ideas presented in this book, the Church is creating an excellent multimedia resource online at lds.org/media-library. I encourage you to explore this site for yourself. For specific ideas on how to use the Church's media site as you learn and teach from Tiny Talks this year, please visit TinyTalksBooks.com.

I hope you will enjoy this book and find many uses for it throughout the year. I am so grateful to my own Church leaders, my friends, and especially my family for the wonderful examples they are to me. I also want to thank the children whose names I borrowed for many of the stories in this book. I know that each one of us is a precious child of a loving Heavenly Father who wants us to remember him in everything we do.

Chapter 1

God Is My Father and He Wants Me to Return to Him

—Romans 8:16

1. My Heavenly Father Cares About Me

Scripture

The Lord hath appeared of old unto me, saying, Yea, I have loved thee with an everlasting love: therefore with loving-kindness have I drawn thee.
—Jeremiah 31:3

Visual Aid:

GAB 116
"Christ and Children from around the World"

Illustration Ideas:

A toy, a family, you doing something you love, Heavenly Father

Think about all the things you love. It could be your favorite toy, the people in your family, or something you love to do. If you love something, you want to know all about it. The things you love are special to you, and you try to take good care of them.

God loves you so much. He knows all about you because you're special to him. He tries to take good care of you. He has given you rules and people to help you so you can stay safe from things that are bad or scary.

We are sons and daughters of God. That's why we call him our Heavenly Father. And because he is our father, he loves us no matter what.

Whenever you're scared or worried, you can talk to Heavenly Father by saying a prayer. He will always hear and answer your prayers. He is the best father you could have.

Thought Question: Who is the father of your body? Who is the father of your spirit?

2. Heavenly Father Has a Plan for Me

One day, a prophet named Samuel came to visit a man named Jesse. God had told Samuel that one of Jesse's sons would be the next king. Samuel asked Jesse to bring his sons so Samuel could meet them.

Jesse's older sons were strong and had learned many things. One of them could have been a great king. But God had someone else in mind. Samuel asked if Jesse had any other sons. Jesse told Samuel that his youngest son, David, was tending the sheep. Samuel asked for David to come inside so Samuel could meet him.

When Samuel saw David, the Spirit told Samuel that David would become the next king. Heavenly Father had a plan for David that no one could have imagined.

Just like David, Heavenly Father has a plan for you that is better than anything you can imagine. He knows who you are, and he knows what will make you happy.

Thought Question: What kinds of things do you think God has planned for your life?

Scripture

But the Lord said unto Samuel, look not on his countenance, or on the height of his stature . . . for man looketh on the outward appearance, but the Lord looketh on the heart.
—1 Samuel 16:7

Visual Aid:

GAB 19
"David Slays Goliath"

Illustration Ideas:

Samuel the prophet, Jesse, Jesse's older sons, David, Heavenly Father

3. Heavenly Father's Plan Will Make Me Happy

Scripture

Adam fell that men might be; and men are, that they might have joy.
—2 Nephi 2:25

Visual Aid:

GAB 60
"Jesus Shows His Wounds"

Illustration Ideas:

A happy face, a sad face, Heavenly Father, Satan, Jesus

Most people like to be happy. It's better to laugh and have fun than to be grumpy and grouchy. The problem is that many people don't know what will really make them happy. They think that having nice things or being the best at something or making others feel bad will make them happier.

Anything can make you happy for a little while, but the only thing that can make you happy forever is following Heavenly Father's plan for you.

Heavenly Father sent us here to earth to learn how to make good choices. He knew we couldn't be really happy until we learned to choose for ourselves. Satan wanted to force us all to choose the right. Heavenly Father and Jesus knew this wouldn't work. We have to make our own choices to do the right things. That's how we can learn to be really happy, now and after we die.

Thought Question: What are some of the blessings that come from following Heavenly Father's plan?

4. My Choices Have Consequences

Jesus told a story about two builders. One built his house on a rock, and the other built his house on sand. Then a storm came along. The house on the sand fell down, but the house on the rock stayed standing.

This story teaches an important lesson about choices. Heavenly Father has given us a gift called agency. Agency means that we have the power to choose for ourselves. But the choices we make still have consequences.

A consequence is something that happens because of something you have chosen. In the story about the builders, the choice was between a strong, rocky foundation or a weak, sandy one. And the consequence was having a house that stayed firm or one that fell down in the storm.

Every choice has a consequence. That's why you need to think carefully before you choose. If you try to make good choices, you'll be blessed with good consequences.

Thought Question: Can you think of some other choices and then identify their consequences?

Scripture

For the power is in them, wherein they are agents unto themselves. And inasmuch as men do good they shall in nowise lose their reward.
—D&C 58:28

Visual Aid:

GAB 39
"The Sermon on the Mount"

Illustration Ideas:

Jesus, two builders, a rock, sand, two houses, a storm, Heavenly Father

Chapter 2

I Came to Earth to Live with God's Children

—Abraham 3:24–25

1. Jesus and Heavenly Father Worked Together to Make the Earth

Scripture

And God saw everything that he had made, and behold it was very good. And the evening and the morning were the sixth day.
—Genesis 1:31

Visual Aid:

GAB 2
"The Lord Created All Things"

Illustration Ideas:

A boy and a girl, a recipe, cookies, Heavenly Father and Jesus, the earth

Hailee and Dustin are in the same class at school. Their teacher gave them a project to do together for homework. For their project, they needed to follow a recipe and bake something yummy.

With their parents' help, Hailee and Dustin measured the ingredients, set the oven to the right temperature, and baked cookies to share with their whole class.

It was fun to work together to make something, but it was hard too. Hailee thought Dustin took too long to measure things, and he thought she wasn't being careful enough.

Heavenly Father and Jesus are the perfect examples of how to work together. When Heavenly Father needed to create an earth for us to live on, he gave Jesus directions. Then Jesus used the directions to create this beautiful world where we can learn and grow. They worked hard to make this the best place for us to live.

Thought Question: Why did Heavenly Father ask Jesus to help him create the earth?

2. Heavenly Father Knows I Will Make Mistakes

Adam and Eve were the first people on the earth. They lived in a beautiful place called the Garden of Eden. Heavenly Father visited them there and gave them many things to eat and enjoy.

Adam and Eve loved it in the Garden of Eden, but one day they had to leave. They had made a mistake. Heavenly Father had asked them not to eat a certain kind of fruit, but Satan tempted Adam and Eve. They ate the fruit, even though they knew they weren't supposed to. This meant they couldn't be in the Garden with Heavenly Father anymore.

Instead, Adam and Eve needed to learn to repent and try harder to be good. Heavenly Father knows we will make mistakes sometimes, but his plan helps us to change. When we try our hardest, Heavenly Father's plan lets us become perfect just like he is.

Thought Question: In Heavenly Father's plan, will we be punished for the mistakes other people make?

Scripture

The natural man is an enemy to God, and has been from the fall of Adam, and will be, forever and ever, unless he yields to the enticings of the Holy Spirit . . . and becometh a saint through the atonement.
—*Mosiah 3:19*

Visual Aid:

GAB 4
"Adam and Eve Kneeling at an Altar"

Illustration Ideas:

Adam and Eve, the Garden of Eden, Heavenly Father, fruit, Satan, Jesus Christ

3. I Came to Earth to Get a Body and Learn to Make Good Choices

Scripture

I know that the Lord giveth no commandments unto the children of men, save he shall prepare a way for them that they may accomplish the thing which he commandeth them.
—1 Nephi 3:7

Visual Aid:

GAB 3
"The Earth"

Illustration Ideas:

A bike, a boy, the earth, the ten commandments, Heavenly Father

T.J. is learning to ride his bike. He already knows how to pedal fast and make sharp turns. He knows it can be a little scary to learn something new. But he also knows that if he tries hard, asks for help when he needs to, and takes it one step at a time, he can do anything.

Heavenly Father sent us to earth so we could learn to do new things. He gave us our bodies so we could learn to take care of them and make good choices. Sometimes life here on earth might seem scary or hard, but when we try to choose the right, Heavenly Father will help us.

The scriptures tell us we can do anything with Heavenly Father's help. He knows how to bless us with exactly the things we need. And he will never give us choices or trials that are too hard for us to figure out. That's because he loves us and wants us to return to him someday.

Thought Question: Why did we all need to come to the earth and gain bodies?

4. I Can Return to Heavenly Father if I Follow His Plan

Ava loves to watch the geese that fly high overhead. In the spring they fly one direction, and in the fall they fly the other way. This is because the geese need to migrate to warmer places in the winter so they won't be cold. Then in the summer they return to the same places they lived before.

All of us here on earth are like geese. We lived in one place before we came to earth, and someday, after we die, we will return to the same place to be with our Heavenly Father. But just like the geese have to work hard to fly all the way home, we need to work hard to do the things our Heavenly Father wants us to do.

When we keep the commandments, we show Heavenly Father that we love him and want to live with him again someday.

Thought Question: How do geese know which direction to go when they migrate? How can we know which way to go on our journey back to Heavenly Father?

Scripture

Blessed are they that do his commandments, that they may have right to the tree of life, and may enter in through the gates into the city.
—*Revelation 22:14*

Visual Aid:

GAB 66
"The Second Coming"

Illustration Ideas:

Geese, a girl, the sky, summer, winter, the earth, Heavenly Father

Chapter 3

Jesus Christ Prepared the Way for Me to Return to God

—D&C 43:34

1. Jesus Taught by Word and Deed

Scripture

Jesus saith unto him, I am the way, the truth, and the life: no man cometh unto the Father, but by me.
—John 14:6

Visual Aid:

GAB 37
"Calling of the Fishermen"

Illustration Ideas:

A boy, football equipment, a book, a TV, a football team, Jesus, the scriptures, a church building, a heart, a happy face

For Trevor, football is the best sport in the whole world. He practices hard all year long so when it's time to play on a team, he can do his best. Trevor likes to read books and listen to people talk about football on TV. But the best way for him to try to get better is by actually watching a good football team play and then trying to do all the same things they do.

This is also true for us. If we want to become better at following Jesus, we can read the scriptures or listen to people talk about him at church. But the best way to be more like Jesus is to do all the same things he did.

Jesus set a perfect example for us to follow. If we try to remember the things he did while he was alive and try to do those same things, we will become more and more like him. We will learn to love people the way he did. And we will be happy like he was.

Thought Question: Why is it so important to try to become more like Jesus?

2. Jesus Suffered So That I Can Live with Heavenly Father Again

Have you ever stayed inside in the dark for a long time and then walked out into the bright sunlight? It takes a few minutes for your eyes to adjust and it can make your head hurt a little bit.

That's how it would feel if you met Heavenly Father before you were ready to see him again. Heavenly Father loves each one of us because we are his children. He wants us to return to live with him again. But even though we might love him too, we wouldn't want to live with him unless we were clean and bright like he is. Otherwise it would hurt us inside to be close to him.

That's why Jesus sacrificed his life for us. He knew we would need a way to become clean and bright again, so he suffered for everything that makes us feel dark and sad. He took away all those things because he wants you to be able to change from darkness to light and live with Heavenly Father again after you die.

Thought Question: How can you use the Atonement to change?

Scripture

I am the light which shineth in the darkness, and the darkness comprehendeth it not.
—*D&C 6:21*

Visual Aid:

GAB 61
"Go Ye Therefore"

Illustration Ideas:

Darkness, light, the sun, Heavenly Father, Jesus

3. I Will Live Again like Jesus

Scripture

And though after my skin worms destroy this body, yet in my flesh shall I see God.
—Job 19:26

Visual Aid:

GAB 59
"Mary and the Resurrected Jesus Christ"

Illustration Ideas:

Jesus, a body and a spirit, the garden tomb, Jesus's disciples

When Jesus lived on the earth, many people were confused about what would happen after they died. They didn't know if they would go somewhere else or just disappear forever. Jesus tried to tell them he would prepare a way for them to live again after they died.

Some people understood, but others were still confused. Then when Jesus was killed, the people were so sad. Three days later, Jesus appeared to his disciples. Even though he had died, his body was alive again. The people were so happy to see Jesus. They finally understood that they could live again after they died because Jesus had overcome death.

Each of us will live again after we die. This is called being resurrected, and it is a marvelous gift from Jesus and Heavenly Father.

Thought Question: What happens to our bodies and our spirits when we die? What happens to them when we are resurrected?

4. My Savior Is Jesus Christ

Saul was a bad man. He tried to hurt the people who believed in Jesus. Then one day as Saul was traveling, Jesus suddenly appeared and told Saul to stop hurting the people in the church.

After that, Saul changed everything about himself. He even changed his name to Paul. Instead of doing bad things, he repented and tried to always do good. He knew Jesus had saved him from feeling yucky and sad. And he knew that it was Jesus's Atonement that let him change.

Paul became a great missionary. He wrote letters that became scriptures, and he helped everyone he could to learn more about Jesus.

Jesus wants to save you from bad and yucky things, just like he saved Paul. When you repent and try to choose good things, you are letting Jesus save you. This means you are letting him become your Savior.

Thought Question: Why do we all need a Savior? What kinds of things does Jesus save us from?

Scripture

I heard a voice speaking unto me, and saying in the Hebrew tongue, Saul, Saul, why persecutest thou me? It is hard for thee to kick against the pricks.
—*Acts 26:14*

Visual Aid:

GAB 56
"Jesus Praying in Gethsemane"

Illustration Ideas:

Saul, Jesus, some disciples, a missionary, the scriptures

17

Chapter 4

The Church of Jesus Christ Is on the Earth Again

—D&C 35:17

1. The True Gospel Was Lost after Jesus Died

Scripture

Behold, they have taken away from the gospel of the Lamb many parts which are plain and most precious; and also many covenants of the Lord they have taken away.
—1 Nephi 13:26

Visual Aid:

GAB 62
"The Ascension of Jesus"

Illustration Ideas:

A boy, a blanket, a park, a car, a house, Jesus, the apostles, Heavenly Father

Griffin loves his favorite blanket. He takes it with him wherever he goes: to the park, in the car, and out in his backyard. Since Griffin is still little and he takes his blanket everywhere, it's easy for his blanket to get lost.

If we lose something special, we do our best to find it. And if we can't, we try to remember what it was like when we had it. That's what happened with the gospel.

After Jesus died, his apostles shared the gospel with everyone. But some people decided to take only parts of the gospel and change the other parts. Over time, the true gospel was lost. The only thing the people could do was try to remember what it was like when they had it.

The people did the best they could, but God knew they would need his help to find the true gospel Jesus had taught. Heavenly Father prepared a plan so that one day, the true church could be restored.

Thought Question: Do you know which parts of the true gospel were lost after Jesus died?

2. Joseph Smith Prayed to Know the Truth

It had been almost two thousand years since Jesus came to the earth. There were many different churches and teachings about what was right and wrong. Joseph Smith wanted to know what was true. He wanted to know if God cared about him. So he prayed.

When Joseph prayed, Jesus and Heavenly Father heard him. They knew Joseph was the right person to bring back the true church. They appeared to Joseph as he was praying. As Joseph grew up, he kept praying and learning more about the true church. Then he shared what he learned with others.

You can experience the same thing Joseph did when you pray. Even though Heavenly Father and Jesus may not appear to you, you can feel the Spirit and know for yourself what is true. And you will find out how much Heavenly Father loves and cares about you.

Thought Question: Why is it important to know the truth about things like the church?

Scripture

It was impossible for a person young as I was, and so unacquainted with men and things, to come to any certain conclusion who was right and who was wrong.
—Joseph Smith—History 1:8

Visual Aid:

GAB 90
"The First Vision"

Illustration Ideas:

Joseph Smith, the Sacred Grove, Heavenly Father and Jesus, a child praying, a heart

3. Angels Appeared to Restore God's Power on the Earth

Scripture

To have the privilege of receiving the mysteries of the kingdom of heaven, to have the heavens opened unto them . . . and to enjoy the communion and presence of God the Father and Jesus the mediator of the new covenant.
—D&C 107:19

Visual Aid:

GAB 94
"Melchizedek Priesthood Restoration"

Illustration Ideas:

Joseph Smith; John the Baptist; Peter, James, and John; Jesus; a priesthood blessing

Have you ever wondered why the true church needed to be restored? There were plenty of churches in Joseph Smith's day. He could have tried to change one of those churches instead of starting a whole new church.

One of the biggest reasons Joseph needed to start a new church had to do with power and authority. Many churches accomplish good things with God's help. But in our church, Heavenly Father has actually given us his power. We call this power the priesthood.

The priesthood was restored by John the Baptist and Peter, James, and John. These are the same people who used the priesthood when Jesus was on the earth. They appeared to Joseph Smith as angels and gave him God's power. With this power, Joseph could do the same things Jesus did when Jesus was alive, like healing the sick, raising the dead, and blessing everyone around him.

Thought Question: What does it mean to have authority and power from God?

4. Because of Joseph Smith, We Have the Fulness of the Gospel

When Joseph Smith was still quite young, he learned about a sacred record that was hidden near his home. An angel named Moroni told Joseph that this record held the full truth about Jesus Christ's church.

But the record had been written long ago, in a language no one understood anymore. Joseph would need some special tools to translate this book. These tools included the Holy Ghost and the Urim and Thummim. With the help of Heavenly Father and these tools, Joseph successfully translated the Book of Mormon.

The Book of Mormon was written a long time ago by prophets in ancient America. Along with the Bible, the Book of Mormon explains exactly what Jesus taught while he was on the earth. Many precious gospel truths that had been lost since Jesus's time were restored when Joseph translated the Book of Mormon.

Thought Question: What tools are available to you to help you know what is true?

Scripture

[Moroni] said there was a book . . . that the fulness of the everlasting Gospel was contained in it . . . and that God had prepared [the Urim and Thummim] for the purpose of translating this book.
—*Joseph Smith—History 1:34–35*

Visual Aid:

GAB 92
"Joseph Smith Translating the Book of Mormon"

Illustration Ideas:

Moroni, Joseph Smith, the Urim and Thummim, the Book of Mormon, the Bible

Chapter 5

We Learn about the Restored Gospel from Prophets

—Amos 3:7

1. Jesus Leads Our Church with Help from Living Prophets

Scripture

We believe in the same organization that existed in the Primitive Church, namely, apostles, prophets, pastors, teachers, evangelists, and so forth.
—Articles of Faith 1:6

Visual Aid:

GAB 38
"Christ Ordaining the Apostles"

Illustration Ideas:

Two girls, a church building, the prophet, apostles, general authorities, Jesus

Elsa has a little sister named Cambria. They like to play together, but sometimes they have a hard time deciding who gets to be the boss. They know it's more fun to play when they can take turns being in charge, but it's hard to remember that all the time.

In our church we always have the same boss. It's Jesus. He is always the leader. But since Jesus doesn't live here on the earth right now, we have other leaders who take care of the church and make sure that we are all doing what Jesus wants us to do.

Jesus knew that just like with Elsa and Cambria, it's sometimes hard for one person to be in charge all the time. That's why Jesus created a church with lots of leaders. Our prophet leads the church, but he has counselors, apostles, and others who help him. When we follow the prophet and his helpers, we are following Jesus Christ.

Thought Question: How does the organization of our church compare to other churches you know about?

2. The Living Prophets Teach Us What We Need to Know Today

The scriptures teach us about lots of different prophets like Adam, Noah, Malachi, Lehi, and Moroni. Each of these prophets was important, and we can learn many lessons from the things they wrote in the scriptures. But the most important prophets for us to learn from are the prophets we have today.

President Monson, his counselors, and the apostles are all prophets. They speak to us at general conference and at other times during the year. Their messages are so important because they are meant especially for us.

Heavenly Father knows us. He knows what is happening all around us, and he inspires our prophets to teach us exactly what we need to know right now.

We can follow the counsel of the living prophets by listening reverently to their messages. We can also talk about their teachings with our families and at church.

Thought Question: What have the living prophets taught you lately?

Scripture

And though the heavens and the earth pass away, my word shall not pass away, but shall all be fulfilled, whether by mine own voice or by the voice of my servants, it is the same.
—D&C 1:38

Visual Aid:

GAB 137
"Thomas S. Monson"

Illustration Ideas:

Ancient prophets, the scriptures, President Monson, the apostles, the conference center

3. I Can Follow the Prophet by Paying My Tithing

After the pioneers traveled to Utah, they needed to build a temple, houses, cities, and roads. Some of the saints had money to do this, but many came from countries far away. They had spent all their money getting to Utah, so when they arrived, they needed help right away.

The prophets knew that great blessings come from paying tithing. They knew Heavenly Father could bless the church with enough money to take care of everyone, but the people would need to obey the law of tithing.

The law of tithing is a way to show Heavenly Father that we know our money and our things don't really belong to us. They belong to Heavenly Father. We can show gratitude for the things he's given us by sharing them with others.

That's how the pioneers built a temple, made such a nice place to live, and cared for those who needed help.

Thought Question: Has your family been blessed for paying tithing?

4. Joseph Smith Taught Us to Live the Word of Wisdom

Natalia's baby brother, Elijah, likes to put everything in his mouth. He even tries to eat dirt, rocks, or other yucky things. Natalia helps Elijah by making sure he doesn't eat things that might make him sick.

Heavenly Father has prepared lots of yummy foods for us to eat. Through the Prophet Joseph Smith, he gave us some special rules about what things we should and should not eat. These rules are called the Word of Wisdom. It teaches us to eat healthy foods that are good for our bodies. It also tells us to stay away from drugs, tobacco, and other things that could make us sick.

When we live the Word of Wisdom, Heavenly Father blesses us. He has promised we will be able to run and not be weary and walk and not faint. This means our bodies will be strong and healthy so we can do all the things he wants us to do.

Thought Question: Why does Heavenly Father want us to take good care of our bodies?

Scripture

And all saints who remember to keep and do these sayings, walking in obedience to the commandments, shall receive health in their navel and marrow to their bones; And shall find wisdom and great treasures of knowledge.
—D&C 89:18–19

Visual Aid:

GAB 87
"Brother Joseph"

Illustration Ideas:

Dirt and rocks, good food, the scriptures, a person running

Chapter 6

Being Baptized and Confirmed Is Part of God's Plan for Me

—3 Nephi 30:2

1. Jesus Was Baptized and I Can Be Too

Scripture

And Philip said, If thou believest with all thine heart, thou mayest. And he answered and said, I believe that Jesus Christ is the Son of God.
—Acts 8:37

Visual Aid:

GAB 35
"John the Baptist Baptizing Jesus"

Illustration Ideas:

Philip, a man, a road, a carriage, the scriptures, Jesus, a person being baptized

One time, an apostle named Philip met a man as they were traveling on a road. The man was reading his scriptures. He asked Philip to sit in his carriage for a while and help him understand the scriptures.

As they talked, Philip taught the man about Jesus. The man believed what Philip said. Then they passed some water. The man asked if he could be baptized. Philip asked if the man really believed in Jesus with his whole heart. The man said he did. So Philip baptized him in the same way Jesus was baptized.

You can be baptized too. Being baptized is an important step in returning to Heavenly Father. In order to be baptized you need to believe in Jesus and in the gospel with your whole heart. When you are baptized in the same way Jesus was, you show Jesus and Heavenly Father that you want to become like them.

Thought Question: Why is it important to be baptized in the same way Jesus was?

2. The Holy Ghost Helps Me to Know What Is Right

Lizzie is always singing nursery rhymes. She often hums them to herself, even when no one is listening. Lizzie knows that songs and music are an important part of our lives. You can't see a song, but it still has power. It can change your mood or make you remember something. It can even help the people around you.

That's how the Holy Ghost is. Even though you can't see the Holy Ghost, he still has power. He helps us know right from wrong.

Our job is to learn how to hear and follow the promptings he gives us. If you practice being still and reverent, even when there are lots of distractions around you, you'll learn to hear the still, small voice of the Holy Ghost. Just like Lizzie sings even when no one is listening, the Holy Ghost is always trying to tell us things. We just need to learn to pay attention.

Thought Question: Has the Holy Ghost ever prompted you to do something? What was that like?

Scripture

Then Peter said unto them, Repent, and be baptized every one of you in the name of Jesus Christ for the remission of sins, and ye shall receive the gift of the Holy Ghost.
—*Acts 2:38*

Visual Aid:

GAB 105
"The Gift of the Holy Ghost"

Illustration Ideas:

A girl, a musical note, the Holy Ghost, a person being reverent

3. Taking the Sacrament Renews My Baptismal Covenants

Scripture

And that thou mayest more fully keep thyself unspotted from the world, thou shalt go to the house of prayer and offer up thy sacraments upon my holy day.
—D&C 59:9

Visual Aid:

GAB 108
"Passing the Sacrament"

Illustration Ideas:

A person, a toy, four seasons, a person being baptized, the sacrament, Heavenly Father

Most things in life are only new once. As time goes on, people get older, toys break, the seasons change, and the things we used to like don't seem as nice anymore.

But that's not true for some things. When we are baptized, we make a special promise with Heavenly Father called a covenant. This promise never has to get old or broken because we can make it new again by renewing it.

We renew our baptismal covenant when we take the sacrament at church. The sacrament is a special time to think about our promise to Heavenly Father and to remember what we need to do to keep that promise.

If you keep trying to remember your covenant, Heavenly Father will bless you. He will keep that promise new and special forever so it never gets old or fades away.

Thought Question: How can you show Heavenly Father that you want to keep your promises to him?

4. I Can Change by Repenting

Dorothea loves to paint. She uses lots of different colors to make her pictures bright and interesting. Sometimes her paintings turn out just the way she imagined them and she's happy to show them to her family and friends. But sometimes she makes mistakes when she's painting, and other times she can't decide how to make her painting look like the thing she's imagining.

Even though we don't all like to paint, each of us is creating something with our lives. And in life, each of us will sometimes make mistakes.

When this happens, we often get frustrated or discouraged. But Jesus has provided the perfect way to change our lives and make them more beautiful. It takes time and hard work to learn how to repent and be forgiven. But with the Savior's help, your life can become more beautiful than anything you could create by yourself.

Thought Question: Is it harder for you to forgive others or yourself? Why?

Scripture

Wherefore, my beloved . . . work out your own salvation with fear and trembling. For it is God which worketh in you both to will and to do of his good pleasure.
—Philippians 2:12–13

Visual Aid:

GAB 104
"Girl Being Baptized"

Illustration Ideas:

A painting, paints, a girl, a family, Jesus, a person smiling

Chapter 7

Heavenly Father's Plan Includes Eternal Families

—"The Family: A Proclamation to the World," paragraph 7

1. Heavenly Father Wanted Me to Be Part of a Family

Scripture

Children, obey your parents in the Lord: for this is right.
—*Ephesians 6:1*

Visual Aid:

A photo of your family

Illustration Ideas:

Ants, lions, fish, a family, Heavenly Father, a house

In nature, many animals like to be together. Ants work together to build their anthills. Lions hunt together. Fish swim together to stay safe from sharks. Even though they can't really think and feel the way we can, many animals like to live together and help each other.

People are the same way. We need each other to be happy. That's why Heavenly Father sent each of us to a family.

Our families are all different. Your family is perfect for you because Heavenly Father knows you and the people in your family. He knows you are the best person to help the people in your family, and he knows that they are the best people to help you.

Families help us to create peace and happiness. They keep us safe from danger. When we try to be kind to the people in our families, we are blessed.

Thought Question: What do you like about your family?

2. My Family Grows Stronger When We Have Righteous Habits

Do you know what a habit is? It's something you do all the time without even thinking about it. Sometimes our habits can be bad or annoying to other people. But once something becomes a habit, it's hard to stop doing it.

That's why we need to make sure our habits are good ones, like saying our prayers and trying to hear the Spirit's still, small voice. Usually we think of a habit as something that just one person does. But a habit could also be something you do as a family.

Some families have a habit of eating dinner together. Some have a habit of playing basketball or watching movies. There are lots of fun things you could do together as a family. But the most important things your family can do are righteous habits, like saying family prayer, reading the scriptures together, and having family home evening.

Thought Question: How can you help your family adopt righteous habits?

Scripture

Successful marriages and families are established and maintained on principles of faith, prayer, . . . love, compassion, work, and wholesome recreational activities.
—*The Family Proclamation, paragraph 7*

Visual Aid:

GAB 112
"Family Prayer"

Illustration Ideas:

A person praying, a family, dinner, a basketball, a TV, scriptures, family home evening

3. My Family Is Blessed by the Priesthood

Scripture

And . . . after my father, Lehi, had spoken unto all his household, according to the feelings of his heart and the Spirit of the Lord which was in him, he waxed old. And it came to pass that he died.
—2 Nephi 4:12

Visual Aid:

GAB 71
"Lehi and His People Arrive in the Promised Land"

Illustration Ideas:

Lehi, Lehi's family in the wilderness, Heavenly Father, a temple, your family

Lehi was a prophet. With Heavenly Father's help, he brought his family from their home in Jerusalem, through the wilderness, and across the ocean to their new home in ancient America. Along the way, Lehi used his priesthood power to help his family know which way to go and to keep them safe.

Before he died, Lehi talked to each of his children. He taught them important things and gave them blessings. He could do this because he had the priesthood.

The priesthood is the same power that Heavenly Father and Jesus used to create the earth. It is the same power we use today to perform baptisms and to seal families together forever. The power of the priesthood can heal people who are sick and comfort those who are sad. Because we have the priesthood today, our families are blessed, just like Lehi's family was blessed.

Thought Question: Who do you know that holds the priesthood? How has it blessed you?

4. I Can Have a Family That Lasts Forever

Finley's mom makes amazing wedding cakes. She uses special tools and then she covers it with a hard kind of frosting that Finley thinks looks like his modeling clay.

He likes to help his mom make cakes, but Finley always knows a wedding cake can't last forever. As soon as one is finished, his mom delivers it so someone can eat it.

Finley knows that someday, his mom wants to make a cake for his wedding. But he also knows that his mom wants him to create something much more important than a cake. His mom wants him to be married in the temple so he can be sealed to his family forever.

There are lots of things, like cake, that are only meant to last for a little while. But a family is meant to last forever, even after we die. That's the kind of family each of us can have if we get married in the temple.

Thought Question: How can you prepare now to be married in the temple someday?

Scripture

If a man marry a wife by . . . the new and everlasting covenant . . . Then shall they be gods, because they have no end; therefore shall they be from everlasting to everlasting.
—D&C 132:19–20

Visual Aid:

GAB 120
"Young Couple Going to the Temple"

Illustration Ideas:

A wedding cake, a boy, the temple, a bride and groom

Chapter 8

I Can Talk with God When I Pray

—D&C 112:10

1. I Can Learn to Pray like Jesus

Scripture

After this manner therefore pray ye: Our Father which art in heaven, Hallowed be thy name.
—Matthew 6:9

Visual Aid:

GAB 33
"Jesus Praying with His Mother"

Illustration Ideas:

Jesus, food, a person praying, Heavenly Father

When Jesus lived on the earth, he taught his followers how to pray. Then he prayed with them to set an example for them.

In his prayer, Jesus prayed to Heavenly Father. He used special words to show reverence. He thanked Heavenly Father for the things Heavenly Father had given him. He then asked for other blessings. Some of the blessings he asked for were physical, like food. Others were spiritual, like forgiveness and protection from Satan. Then Jesus said that he only wanted those blessings if that was what Heavenly Father wanted too.

After Jesus finished praying, he reminded the people that Heavenly Father could only bless them with the things they needed if they were kind to others and obeyed the commandments. Jesus set a perfect example of how to pray.

Thought Question: Why do we pray in the name of Jesus Christ?

2. I Can Pray Always

The scriptures teach us that we should pray always. This means that instead of praying only at church or only when you really need something, you can pray anywhere you go and anytime you want to.

Sometimes you'll be in places where it might seem strange to pray. If you feel funny speaking your prayer out loud, you can say the words in your mind instead. This is called a silent prayer, and Heavenly Father will still hear you praying, even if you don't pray out loud.

We should always have a prayer in our hearts. This means even when you aren't saying a prayer, you can keep your thoughts and feelings clean and pure so the Spirit can be with you.

If you pray always, you can feel the Spirit all the time. The Spirit will help you make good choices and keep you safe from danger and from bad thoughts or actions.

Thought Question: What kinds of things should you say in your prayers?

Scripture

Watch ye therefore, and pray always, that ye may be accounted worthy to escape all these things that shall come to pass, and to stand before the Son of man.
—*Luke 21:36*

Visual Aid:

GAB 111
"Young Boy Praying"

Illustration Ideas:

A person praying, a church, a heart, the Spirit, Heavenly Father

3. Heavenly Father Always Answers My Prayers

Scripture

And she was a widow of about fourscore and four years, which departed not from the temple, but served God with fastings and prayers night and day.
—*Luke 2:37*

Visual Aid:

GAB 32
"Simeon Reverencing the Christ Child"

Illustration Ideas:

Anna, the temple, baby Jesus, Joseph and Mary, a person praying, Heavenly Father

Anna spent her whole life serving in the temple. One time when she was praying, she learned she would see Jesus someday. Anna continued to pray and fast. She looked forward to seeing Jesus for herself.

When Anna was very old, Joseph and Mary brought the baby Jesus to the temple where Anna worked. It had taken a long time for Anna's prayers to be answered, but she was so grateful and happy to see Jesus. Even though he was only a baby, Anna knew that one day Jesus would save us all from our sins. She told everyone about Jesus and the great works he would do someday.

Sometimes when we pray, we get an answer right away. Other times it takes longer. That doesn't mean we should stop praying. No matter what, Heavenly Father will always answer your prayers. You just need to have faith that he loves you and knows what is best for you.

Thought Question: What are some ways your prayers have been answered?

4. I Can Learn to Recognize Personal Revelation

Colby's parents speak different languages. His mom grew up in Brazil, so she speaks Portuguese. His dad served a mission in Germany, so he speaks German. Colby has learned both languages, and he speaks English too. But there's another language Colby is still learning: the language of the Spirit.

We all need to learn this language so we will know what Heavenly Father wants us to do. When we pray, the Spirit helps us hear and understand the answers Heavenly Father sends us.

Sometimes the Spirit speaks with a warm, peaceful feeling when you're doing what's right. Sometimes the Spirit directs you to scriptures that answer your questions. And sometimes the Spirit sends other people to answer your prayers. When you recieve an answer through the Spirit, you are receiving personal revelation.

Thought Question: How can you learn to recognize the language of the Spirit?

Scripture

It was not a harsh voice, neither was it a loud voice; nevertheless, and notwithstanding it being a small voice it did pierce them that did hear to the center . . . and did cause their hearts to burn.
—3 Nephi 11:3

Visual Aid:

Your scriptures

Illustration Ideas:

A boy, a map, words in a different language, the Spirit, the scriptures, a person praying, a happy face

Chapter 9

Heavenly Father Wants Me to Serve Him Always

—D&C 59:5

1. I Can Follow Jesus by Serving Others

Scripture

But charity is the pure love of Christ, and it endureth forever; and whoso is found posessed of it at the last day, it shall be well with him.
—Moroni 7:47

Visual Aid:

GAB 47
"Christ and the Children"

Illustration Ideas:

Jesus, a crowd of people, some children, a heart

Jesus only had a short time to live on the earth. He had lots of things he needed to teach us. But one of the most important lessons he wanted us to learn was that we need to serve each other. Even though he was busy, Jesus spent most of his time blessing other people. He was never too busy to help someone who needed him.

One time after Jesus had been teaching for a while, some people brought their young children to see Jesus. The other people who were listening to Jesus were angry. They said that Jesus wouldn't want to see the children.

Jesus wasn't angry. He told everyone who was listening that children are special. Jesus loves each of us. He is always ready to help us because he wants us to be happy.

That is how we should feel about other people. As we follow the example Jesus set and try to serve others, we will learn to love others too.

Thought Question: Do you know what charity means? Why do we need to have charity?

2. I Can Follow the Prophet by Serving Others

President Monson is our living prophet today. He and his apostles are all good examples of how to serve others. Even though they are very busy and have lots of work to do, they still take time to serve others.

Instead of worrying about himself, President Monson is always worried about the people around him. When he was a young man, he was asked to serve as a bishop in a large ward. This was a big job for such a young person. But President Monson knew that if he focused on helping people, Heavenly Father would help him too.

Jesus taught us to think of others before ourselves because putting yourself first will actually make you more miserable than if you forget all about yourself and serve other people instead. President Monson is a good example of someone who focuses on others before himself, and you can do that too.

Thought Question: What could you do this week to put the needs of others before your own needs?

Scripture

For whosoever will save his life shall lose it; but whosoever shall lose his life for my sake and the gospel's, the same shall save it.
—*Mark 8:35*

Visual Aid:

GAB 137
"Thomas S. Monson"

Illustration Ideas:

President Monson, Jesus, a bishop, a happy face, a crowd of people

3. When I Serve Others, I Am Serving Heavenly Father

Scripture

When ye are in the service of your fellow beings ye are only in the service of your God.
—Mosiah 2:17

Visual Aid:

GAB 115
"Service"

Illustration Ideas:

A boy, a package, an email or computer, grandparents, a map, missionary nametags, Heavenly Father

Toby's grandparents just left to serve a mission. It's fun to send them packages and emails, but sometimes Toby wishes they had stayed home so he could see them and play with them.

Before they left, Toby's grandfather told Toby why they were going to serve a mission. His grandfather explained that when we serve other people, we're actually serving Heavenly Father. This means Toby's grandparents are serving people in a different country, and at the same time, they're also serving Heavenly Father.

Heavenly Father loves it when we serve others. He will bless us for being helpful and loving. It is exactly the sort of thing he would do if he were here on the earth.

Toby misses his grandparents, but he knows how important it is to give service, and he's grateful his grandparents want to help other people.

Thought Question: What are some ways you have served others in the past?

4. I Can Help Jesus by Loving and Serving Others

Joseph Smith needed to translate the Book of Mormon, but he couldn't do it by himself. He prayed for help. One day a man came to see Joseph. The man said his name was Oliver Cowdery and that he had been staying with Joseph's family in a different state. Oliver said that he had come to meet Joseph and find out more about the true gospel.

Oliver soon learned for himself that Joseph was telling the truth. Since Oliver was a schoolteacher, it was easy for him to write down the words Joseph spoke as Joseph translated the Book of Mormon.

Heavenly Father answered Joseph's prayer for help by sending Oliver to help him translate. The same thing still happens today. As you do service for others, you will be helping them and you will be helping Jesus Christ. You may even be the answer to someone else's prayer.

Thought Question: What could you do to serve someone around you?

Scripture

Wherefore, thy soul shall be blessed, and thou shalt dwell safely . . . and thy days shall be spent in the service of thy God. Wherefore I know that thou art redeemed.
—2 Nephi 2:3

Visual Aid:

GAB 92
"Joseph Smith Translating the Book of Mormon"

Illustration Ideas:

Joseph Smith, Oliver Cowdery, the Book of Mormon, Jesus, someone giving service

Chapter 10

I Can Share the Gospel with Everyone

—Matthew 5:16

1. My Example Makes Me a Missionary

Scripture

Let your light so shine before men, that they may see your good works, and glorify your Father which is in heaven.
—Matthew 5:16

Visual Aid:

GAB 66
"The Second Coming"

Illustration Ideas:

A map of the world, a church, a missionary nametag, a light, Jesus Christ

Did you know that in some countries it's illegal to preach the gospel? If you live in one of these places, you are not allowed to talk about your religion. Sometimes you aren't even allowed to worship with other church members.

So how could you be a missionary in a place like that? Easy. You could share the gospel through your example. When others saw how you lived and how happy you were, it would make them want to learn about Jesus Christ.

The same thing is true wherever you live. You can share your testimony and be a missionary just by being a good example. Jesus taught that we should let our lights shine so others see our good works and glorify Heavenly Father. This means that being a good example is one of the best ways to be a good missionary.

Thought Question: Can you think of some ways to set a good example so you can be a missionary?

2. When I Make Good Choices, I Am Being a Missionary

McKay loves to see the missionaries when they come over for dinner. He knows that they are working hard to share the gospel. Someday when he grows up, he wants to serve a mission too.

Missionaries are special people called by God to spread the gospel. Missionaries give up their time and leave their families to serve other people they don't even know. It takes a lot of dedication to be a missionary. You have to keep making good choices, even when it's hard.

McKay knows he can practice being a missionary now by choosing the right, even when it seems hard. He can be reverent in church and learn to feel the Spirit. He can pray every day and listen when his parents read scripture stories. When he makes a mistake, he can repent and try harder to be good. Making good choices now will help McKay be a better missionary now and when he grows up.

Thought Question: What could you do now to practice being a good missionary?

Scripture

Therefore, blessed are ye if ye continue in my goodness, a light unto the Gentiles, and through this priesthood, a savior unto my people Israel
—D&C 86:11

Visual Aid:

GAB 109
"Missionaries: Elders"

Illustration Ideas:

The missionaries, a nametag, a boy praying, a church, the scriptures

For I did liken all scriptures unto us, that it might be for our profit and learning.
—1 Nephi 19:23

Visual Aid:

GAB 70
"Nephi Subdues His Rebellious Brothers"

Illustration Ideas:

Nephi, Nephi's family, tents, the Brass Plates, Laman and Lemuel

3. I Can Be a Missionary to My Family and Friends

Sometimes we think we need to go far away to be missionaries. But that wasn't true for Nephi.

Nephi came from a big family. Even though he wasn't the oldest, Nephi knew he could be a leader and a good example. As his family traveled through the wilderness with their friends, Nephi tried to tell them how he felt about the gospel. When the people around him lost hope, he worked even harder to help them.

He loved to read the scriptures, and he used the Brass Plates to teach his family about the gospel. He tried to help his wicked brothers understand how to pray so they could get answers to their questions.

Nephi was a great missionary. He didn't need to travel far away from his friends and family to serve a mission. His mission was to help the people around him to know and love Heavenly Father.

Thought Question: Why is it important to be a good missionary to your friends and family?

4. My Testimony Grows When I Share It

Ammon and his brothers were mean. They made fun of people who belonged to the church. Then one day, an angel came to visit them and tell them to change. Ammon and his brothers repented.

Ammon knew that he would need to try extra hard to keep his testimony strong so he wouldn't become a bad person again. He and his brothers decided to go on a mission to the Lamanites.

As Ammon shared his testimony with the Lamanites, his testimony grew. He became a powerful missionary. Many Lamanites joined the church after Ammon and his brothers taught them the truth.

Just like Ammon, you can help your testimony become stronger by sharing it with other people. You can share your testimony at church, at school, or wherever you go.

Thought Question: How has sharing your testimony made it stronger?

Scripture

I will not boast of myself, but I will boast of my God, for in his strength I can do all things; yea, behold, many mighty miracles we have wrought in this land, for which we will praise his name forever.
—Alma 26:12

Visual Aid:

GAB 78
"Ammon Defends the Flocks of King Lamoni"

Illustration Ideas:

Ammon, his brothers, an angel, the Lamanites, a missionary, a church building, a school

Chapter 11

We Should Be Grateful

—Mosiah 18:23

1. My Body Is a Sacred Gift from Heavenly Father

Scripture

And the spirit and the body are the soul of man.
—D&C 88:15

Visual Aid:

GAB 119
"Salt Lake Temple"

Illustration Ideas:

A body, a temple, healthy foods, modest clothes, a person playing or exercising, a person sleeping, water, Heavenly Father

The scriptures teach us that our bodies are temples. This means that they can be as beautiful and special to us as temples are. Everyone has a different body, but you only get one body, so you need to take good care of it.

We can treat our bodies like temples when we eat good, nourishing foods that will help us to be healthy and strong. We also need to keep our bodies clean by making good choices and by dressing modestly. Our bodies need playtime, exercise, sleep, and plenty of water.

Our parents help us to take care of our bodies, but it is our job to make sure they stay healthy so we can do all the things Heavenly Father wants us to do while we are alive.

We should show Heavenly Father that we are grateful for our bodies by making good, healthy choices. When we take care of our bodies, Heavenly Father is pleased.

Thought Question: Why do you think we all have different bodies?

2. I Can Be Grateful for the Things All Around Me

Issy loves to play outside on her swing. As she swings back and forth, she likes to look up in the sky. There are lots of things to see up there: trees, birds, airplanes, and clouds. There are so many things in the world to see and hear and discover.

God created a beautiful world for us. He continues to bless us with the things our bodies need to stay healthy. In fact, if you think about it, everything around you is a blessing from God.

Issy's swing is a blessing because it makes her happy. The trees are a blessing because they make the world beautiful and clean. The airplanes are a blessing because they let us travel quickly from one place to another. As you learn to notice all the blessings around you, you can remember to thank Heavenly Father for everything he has given you.

Thought Question: Why do we sometimes forget to be grateful for the things around us?

Scripture

Live in thanksgiving daily, for the many mercies and blessings which he doth bestow upon you.
—*Alma 34:38*

Visual Aid:

GAB 3
"The Earth"

Illustration Ideas:

A girl, a swing, the sky, trees, birds, airplanes, clouds, Heavenly Father

3. I Can Be Grateful for Spiritual Things

Scripture

And all these gifts come by the Spirit of Christ; and they come unto every man severally, according as he will. And I would exhort you . . . that ye remember that every good gift cometh of Christ.
—Moroni 10:17–18

Visual Aid:

GAB 112
"Family Prayer"

Illustration Ideas:

The world, a person teaching, Jesus, Heavenly Father

There's an expression that goes, "Out of sight, out of mind." It means that when you can't see something, it's easy to forget all about it. This can be true for us too.

The world around us is filled with beautiful and exciting things. When we see the blessings around us, it's pretty easy to thank Heavenly Father for them. But what about the blessings we can't see? These are called spiritual blessings or gifts of the spirit. They include things like being able to teach others, having a lot of faith, and working miracles.

We can't see spiritual gifts like we can see physical gifts, but they are still great blessings in our lives. We need to remember to thank Heavenly Father for our spiritual blessings, just like we thank him for all of the other blessings he gives us. And one of the best ways to thank Heavenly Father for your spiritual gifts is to share those gifts with others.

Thought Question: What do you think your spiritual gifts are?

4. I Can Say Thank You to Heavenly Father

One time a group of ten men came to see Jesus. The men wanted Jesus to heal them because they had a sickness called leprosy. It made their skin look yucky and it hurt a lot.

Jesus said he would heal them. He told the men to go show themselves to the priests. As they were walking toward the priests, they noticed that their skin was healed. Jesus had performed a miracle.

Most of the men were so excited they forgot to say thank you. But one man came back. He shouted for joy. He was so grateful that Jesus had made him better.

Sometimes we are so excited by all the great things around us that we forget to thank Heavenly Father for giving them to us. Even when you are busy or excited, it's important to remember that Heavenly Father wants us to thank him for all of our blessings. We can thank Heavenly Father each time we pray.

Thought Question: Besides saying prayers, how else can you thank Heavenly Father for your blessings?

Scripture

And one of them, when he saw that he was healed, turned back, and with a loud voice glorified God, And fell down on his face at his feet, giving him thanks.
—Luke 17:15–16

Visual Aid:

GAB 46
"The Ten Lepers"

Illustration Ideas:

Ten men, Jesus, one man, Heavenly Father, a person praying

Chapter 12

Someday Jesus Christ Will Return to the Earth

—Job 19:25

1. Ancient Prophets Testified That Jesus Would Come

Scripture

Declare his glory among the heathen: his marvellous works among all nations.
—1 Chronicles 16:24

Visual Aid:

GAB 75
"Abinadi Before King Noah"

Illustration Ideas:

Abinadi, King Noah, Jesus, Alma

Abinadi was a brave prophet. He lived in a wicked place, led by an evil king named Noah. Heavenly Father told Abinadi to preach about Jesus, even though Heavenly Father knew many of the people wouldn't listen.

Abinadi obeyed. He told everyone Jesus would come to the earth and visit the people in America. The people got mad when Abinadi told them to repent. They tied him up and took him to King Noah. The king and his wicked priests tried to trick Abinadi by telling him he was wrong about Jesus.

But Abinadi knew he wasn't wrong. His testimony stayed strong, even when the priests threatened to hurt him. Later Abinadi was killed because he refused to deny what he knew about Jesus Christ. But one of King Noah's priests, named Alma, repented because of Abinadi's testimony. Alma spent the rest of his life teaching others about Jesus, just as Abinadi had taught him.

Thought Question: Can you think of any other prophets who testified of Jesus before he was born?

2. One Day Jesus Will Return to the Earth

When Wyatt's parents leave him with a babysitter, he often gets nervous. His parents tell him that they'll be right back and tell him not to worry. But Wyatt still doesn't like it when they go. He's always happy to see them again when they return.

After Jesus died, his disciples were worried just like Wyatt. They didn't know if Jesus would ever return to help them again. Even today, many people wonder if Jesus will ever return to the earth. Jesus told us not to worry. In the scriptures, Jesus has made it clear that one day he will return again to the earth.

When Jesus comes again, everyone will know who he is. We will be so excited to see him, and he will be excited to see us too. We can prepare for Jesus to come again by keeping the commandments and sharing the gospel with others.

Thought Question: What kinds of things will happen before Jesus comes again?

Scripture

For I will reveal myself from heaven with power and great glory, with all the hosts thereof, and dwell in righteousness with men on earth.
—D&C 29:11

Visual Aid:

GAB 66
"The Second Coming"

Illustration Ideas:

A boy, his parents, a babysitter, Jesus

3. I Want to Live with Heavenly Father Again

Scripture

Who shall ascend into the hill of the Lord? or who shall stand in his holy place? He that hath clean hands, and a pure heart.
—Psalms 24:3–4

Visual Aid:

GAB 120
"Young Couple Going to the Temple"

Illustration Ideas:

The temple, a wedding dress, a girl, Heavenly Father, heaven, Jesus Christ

Lulu loves to look at pictures of the temple. Her parents got married there, and someday she wants to get married there too in a beautiful dress. The temple is a special place where we can feel the spirit. When we go to the temple, we are going to Heavenly Father's house. It's almost like we go to heaven just for a little while.

Someday, after we die, each us will have the chance to return to heaven and live there forever. But that means we need to get ready now.

Jesus taught us how to prepare for heaven. He said we need to love other people. We need to keep the commandments. And we need to make sure Heavenly Father and Jesus are the most important people in our lives.

Lulu knows that everything she does now to help her prepare to go to the temple will also help her prepare to live with Heavenly Father again someday in heaven.

Thought Question: What makes someone worthy to go to the temple?

4. I Know I Am a Child of God

Moses lived long ago. God called him to become a prophet and to lead the people to the promised land. Moses was blessed for being obedient.

One time when Moses went up into the mountains to pray, he had a beautiful vision of all the things that had happened before the earth was created. Then Moses saw everything that would happen on the earth.

After this vision, Satan appeared to try to tempt Moses. But Moses knew that God was his father. Moses used God's power to command Satan to leave. This worked because God is much more powerful than Satan.

We can follow the example Moses set. When we are tempted to do bad things, we can remember that God is our Father, and he is more powerful than Satan. Our Heavenly Father loves us. He will help and protect us whenever we need him because we are his children.

Thought Question: When you are tempted, why does it help to remember that you are a child of God?

Scripture

Nevertheless, calling upon God, he received strength, and he commanded, saying: Depart from me, Satan, for this one God only will I worship, which is the God of glory.
—*Moses 1:20*

Visual Aid:

GAB 13
"Moses and the Burning Bush"

Illustration Ideas:

Moses, the promised land, mountains, the earth, Satan, Heavenly Father

Song Ideas

The following is a list of songs from the Children's Songbook and the adult hymn book that correspond to each talk. You can use them to reinforce the concepts taught in Primary that week. If your musical abilities are limited or you don't have access to an instrument, all of these songs are available at lds.org/music. You can also find additional song ideas and other resources at TinyTalksBooks.com.

Chapter 1

1. I Am a Child of God, 2
   My Heavenly Father Loves Me, 228
   God's Love, 97
   Where Love Is, 138
2. I Will Follow God's Plan, 164
   Families Can Be Together Forever, 188
3. The Church of Jesus Christ, 77
   Choose the Right Way, 160
   I Need My Heavenly Father, 18
   Smiles, 267a
4. Listen, Listen, 107

I Want to Live the Gospel, 148
The Wise Man and the Foolish Man, 281

Chapter 2

1. I Think the World Is Glorious, 230
   Beautiful Savior, 62
   The World Is So Lovely, 233
2. Follow the Prophet (verse 1), 110
   The Second Article of Faith, 122b
   Help Me, Dear Father, 99
3. The Lord Gave Me a Temple, 153
   Head, Shoulders, Knees, and Toes, 275a
   My Heavenly Father Loves Me, 228
   Nephi's Courage, 120
   I Have Two Little Hands, 272
4. Faith, 96
   I Lived in Heaven, 4
   Teach Me to Walk in the Light, 177

Chapter 3

1. Tell Me the Stories of Jesus, 57
   I'm Trying to Be like Jesus, 78
   I'll Walk with You, 140
2. He Sent His Son, 34

The Third Article of Faith, 123
The Lord Is My Light (*Hymns*), 89
3. Did Jesus Really Live Again?, 64
Easter Hosanna, 68
On a Golden Springtime, 88
4. The Sacrament, 72
I Feel My Savior's Love, 74

Chapter 4
1. I Think When I Read That Sweet Story, 56
Follow the Prophet (verse 9), 110
2. The Sacred Grove, 87
An Angel Came to Joseph Smith, 86a
This Is My Beloved Son (verse 3), 76
3. The Priesthood Is Restored, 89
A Young Man Prepared, 166
Love Is Spoken Here, 190
4. The Golden Plates, 86
Book of Mormon Stories, 118
The Eighth Article of Faith, 127
We'll Bring the World His Truth, 172

Chapter 5
1. The Sixth Article of Faith, 126a

Latter-day Prophets, 134
The Church of Jesus Christ, 77

2. Follow the Prophet, 110
Keep the Commandments, 146
Seek the Lord Early, 108

3. I'm Glad to Pay a Tithing, 150a
I Want to Give the Lord My Tenth, 150b
Count Your Blessings (*Hymns*), 241

4. The Lord Gave Me a Temple, 153
The Word of Wisdom, 154

Chapter 6

1. When I Am Baptized, 103
Baptism, 100
When Jesus Christ Was Baptized, 102
I Like My Birthdays, 104

2. Listen, Listen, 107
The Still Small Voice, 106
Search, Ponder, and Pray, 109

3. Before I Take the Sacrament, 73a
To Think about Jesus, 71

4. I Love to See the Temple, 95
Repentance, 98

I Want to Live the Gospel, 148
When I Am Baptized, 103

Chapter 7

1. Families Can Be Together Forever, 188
   Because God Loves Me, 234
   I Have a Family Tree, 199
   Birds in the Tree, 241
2. Family Prayer, 189
   Family Night, 195
   Here We Are Together, 261
3. Love Is Spoken Here, 190
   Fathers, 209
   My Dad, 211
4. I Love to See the Temple, 95
   Families Can Be Together Forever, 188
   I Am a Child of God, 2

Chapter 8

1. I Pray in Faith, 14
   Reverently, Quietly, 26
   We Bow Our Heads, 25a
2. I Love to Pray, 25b
   Search, Ponder, and Pray, 109

Secret Prayer (*Hymns*), 144
3. A Child's Prayer, 12
   Faith, 96
4. The Still Small Voice, 106
   The Ninth Article of Faith, 128a
   Let the Holy Spirit Guide (*Hymns*), 143
   Nephi's Courage, 120

Chapter 9

1. Jesus Said Love Everyone, 61
   Love One Another, 136
   Jesus Loved the Little Children, 59
   I'll Walk with You, 140
2. "Give," Said the Little Stream, 236
   When We're Helping, 198b
   Jesus Wants Me for a Sunbeam, 60
3. Where Love Is, 138
   Go the Second Mile, 167
   Can a Little Child like Me?, 9
4. I Will Be Valiant, 162
   A Happy Helper, 197a
   Mother, I Love You, 207
   I'm Trying to Be like Jesus, 78

Chapter 10

1. I Am like a Star, 163
   The Things I Do, 170
   Shine On, 144
   Dare to Do Right, 158
2. Choose the Right (*Hymns*), 239
   Quickly I'll Obey, 197b
   Seek the Lord Early, 108
   I Hope They Call Me on a Mission, 169
3. I Want to Be a Missionary Now, 168
   Friends Are Fun, 262
   Nephi's Courage, 120
4. Book of Mormon Stories (verse 5), 118
   We'll Bring the World His Truth, 172

Chapter 11

1. Healthy, Wealthy, and Wise, 280
   For Health and Strength, 21a
   The Word of Wisdom, 154
2. All Things Bright and Beautiful, 231
   A Song of Thanks, 20a
   Children All Over the World, 16
   I Think the World Is Glorious, 230

3. Thanks to Thee, 6
   I Thank Thee, Dear Father, 7
   God's Love, 97
4. For Thy Bounteous Blessings, 21b
   Can a Little Child Like Me?, 9
   I Am Glad for Many Things, 151

Chapter 12

1. Book of Mormon Stories (verse 4), 118
   Follow the Prophet, 110
   Samuel Tells of the Baby Jesus, 36
   It Came upon the Midnight Clear (*Hymns*), 207
2. When He Comes Again, 82
   Had I Been a Child, 80
3. I Am a Child of God, 2
   Teach Me to Walk in the Light, 177
   When I Am Baptized, 103
4. Mother, Tell Me the Story, 204
   I Lived in Heaven, 4
   The Church of Jesus Christ, 77
   I Will Follow God's Plan, 164

Additional Ideas

_____

_____

_____

_____

_____

_____

_____

_____

_____

_____

_____

_____

_____

_____

_____

_____

About the Author

Heidi Doxey graduated from Brigham Young University in 2008. Her favorite part of Primary was always singing time, and she still enjoys singing—mostly as a harmony part to her car stereo.

When she's not writing, Heidi enjoys riding her giant pink bicycle around town. Her other favorite pastimes include pretending to be good at volleyball, playing at the park, and reading storybooks in silly voices.

She lives in idyllic northern California and currently splits her time between working as a freelance writer and editor and a nanny.

0 26575 11411 9